Learning Musical Instruments

Should I Play the
Piano?

Nicola Barber

Heinemann Library
Chicago, Illinois

Customer Service 888-454-2279
Visit our website at www.heinemannraintree.com

Designed by Richard Parker and Manhattan Design
Illustrations by Jeff Edwards
Printed and bound in China by Leo Paper Group

11 10 09 08 07
10 9 8 7 6 5 4 3 2 1

Library of Congress Cataloging-in-Publication Data
Barber, Nicola.
  Should I play the piano? / Nicola Barber.
    p. cm. -- (Learning musical instruments)
  Includes bibliographical references and index.
  ISBN 1-4034-8189-X (library binding - hardcover)
  1. Piano--Juvenile literature. I. Title. II. Series.
  ML650.B36 2006
  786.2--dc22   2006006674

Acknowledgments
The publishers would like to thank the following for permission to reproduce photographs:
Alamy pp. **7** (Lebrecht Music and Arts Photo Library), **15**, **17** (Lebrecht Music and Arts Photo Library), **21** (Lebrecht Music and Arts Photo Library), **27** (Imageshop); Corbis pp. **4** (Philip Gould), **6** (Francis G. Mayer), **14** (Kim Sayer), **18** (Bettmann); Eyewire pp. **8**, **9**; Getty Images pp. **16** (Jo Hale), **19** (Carlos Alvarez), **23**; Harcourt Education Ltd/Tudor Photography pp. **5**, **12**, **13**, **24**; Lebrecht p. **26** (Nigel Luckhurst); Redfern pp. **22** (David Redferns), **20** (PALM/RSCH); Superstock p. **25**.

Cover image of Chris Martin of Coldplay playing the piano reproduced with permission of Capital Pictures.

The publishers would like to thank Teryl Dobbs for her assistance in the preparation of this book.

Author dedication: Thanks to my mum, who taught me to play the piano.

Contents

Any words appearing in the text in bold, **like this**, are explained in the Glossary.

Why Do People Play Musical Instruments?

Ever since early humans made simple instruments from pieces of wood or bone, people have loved to make musical noises. Everyone can enjoy making music and listening to it. Music allows people to express their feelings, whether they are happy, sad, playful, or solemn.

People learn to play musical instruments for many different reasons. Some want to learn a new skill. Some want to make music with other players. A few people are able to make a living from playing or teaching. Others play just for pleasure in their spare time. Best of all, music brings people together—at pop concerts, in the concert hall, or playing with friends.

A pianist performs alongside his fellow street musicians in New Orleans.

There are thousands of different musical instruments played by people around the world. In this book, you can find out about one of these instruments: the piano. People everywhere recognize the piano's black-and-white **keyboard** and its special sound. The piano is one of the best-loved instruments of all, and for good reason!

Why play the piano?

The piano can be used in many different ways. People can play keyboards in a pop band.

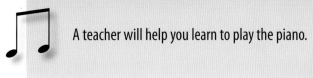

A teacher will help you learn to play the piano.

Others play **jazz** piano. The piano can be a **solo** instrument or it can **accompany** singers or other players. People who can play the piano may also learn to play similar instruments, such as the **organ**, **harpsichord**, or **synthesizer**. People cannot pick up a piano and play it while walking, though, so it does not work in marching bands!

FROM THE EXPERTS

"The piano is able to communicate the subtlest universal truths by means of wood, metal, and **vibrating** air."
Kenneth Miller

What Is a Piano?

The piano is a musical instrument with a **keyboard**. To play the piano, a person presses the keys with his or her fingers. Hammers inside the piano strike strings that **vibrate**, producing sound.

"Soft and loud"

The piano is related to an older keyboard instrument called the **harpsichord**. When a harpsichord player presses a key, a small tab called a plectrum **plucks** a string. No matter how hard or gently the key is pressed, the plectrum plucks the string with the same force. This means that the **volume** of the sound is always the same.

This piano was built by the first piano-maker, Bartolomeo Cristofori.

FROM THE EXPERTS

"A smasher of pianos."

Clara Schumann (see page 20) describing the playing of Franz Liszt

In the early 1700s, an Italian harpsichord-maker named Bartolomeo Cristofori invented a new **mechanism**. A hammer struck a string and then rebounded, allowing the string to vibrate. Now, players could alter the volume by pressing the keys harder or softer. Cristofori's instrument was called *gravicembalo col piano e forte*, meaning "harpsichord with soft and loud." It became known as the fortepiano or pianoforte.

Cristofori's mechanism still provides the basic design used in pianos today. Later piano-makers such as John Broadwood and Sébastien Érard continued to develop the design during the 18th and 19th centuries. The grand piano (see page 9) was developed and used mostly for concerts, but people also wanted to play the piano at home. The upright piano—which took up less space than the grand piano—was developed especially for this purpose. Modern-day alternatives to the traditional piano include electric and **digital** pianos. (See more about these instruments on page 16.)

The pianoforte was soon a big hit with **composers**, players, and audiences.

What are the different parts called?

The piano is a large, complicated instrument. Its many parts are made from different materials. This picture shows a grand piano with the strings held **horizontally** in their metal frame.

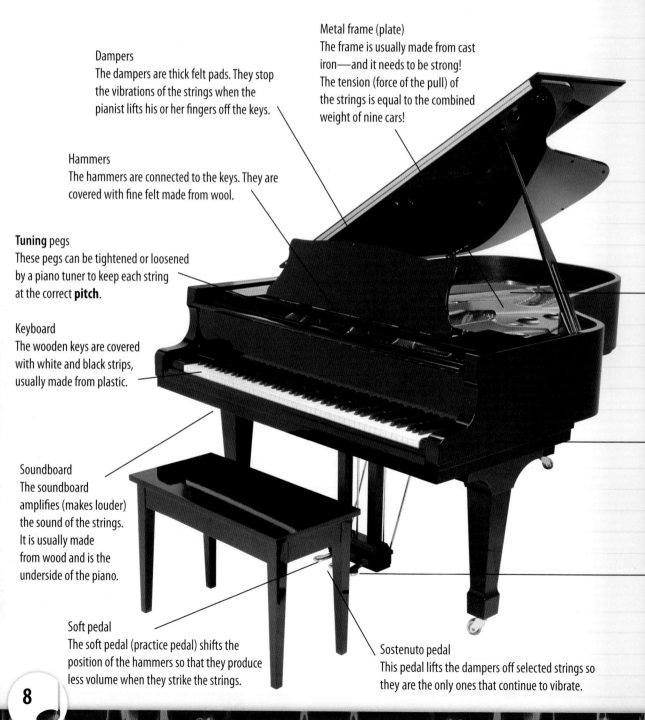

Dampers
The dampers are thick felt pads. They stop the vibrations of the strings when the pianist lifts his or her fingers off the keys.

Hammers
The hammers are connected to the keys. They are covered with fine felt made from wool.

Tuning pegs
These pegs can be tightened or loosened by a piano tuner to keep each string at the correct **pitch**.

Keyboard
The wooden keys are covered with white and black strips, usually made from plastic.

Soundboard
The soundboard amplifies (makes louder) the sound of the strings. It is usually made from wood and is the underside of the piano.

Metal frame (plate)
The frame is usually made from cast iron—and it needs to be strong! The tension (force of the pull) of the strings is equal to the combined weight of nine cars!

Soft pedal
The soft pedal (practice pedal) shifts the position of the hammers so that they produce less volume when they strike the strings.

Sostenuto pedal
This pedal lifts the dampers off selected strings so they are the only ones that continue to vibrate.

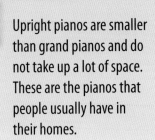

Upright pianos are smaller than grand pianos and do not take up a lot of space. These are the pianos that people usually have in their homes.

Strings
Piano strings are made from high-quality steel. Strings for the lower notes are also wound with copper. Each high note uses three strings, the middle notes use two strings, and the lowest notes have one string. Every piano has 215 to 230 strings. These range in length from 2 inches (5 cm) to more than 83 inches (210 cm). "Overstringing" saves space by crossing the strings over each other.

Case
The case protects everything inside. It is usually made of wood.

Damper pedal
The damper pedal lifts the dampers off all the strings so that they vibrate longer.

PIANO FACTS: Grand pianos

The frame of the grand piano is horizontal rather than vertical. Small grand pianos, called "baby grands," are about 5.6 feet (1.7 meters) long. Full-length "concert" grands are up to 10 feet (3 meters) long. The concert grand's open lid helps to project (send out) the piano's sound across the concert hall.

How Does a Piano Make Its Sound?

The sound of the piano comes from **vibrating** strings. The movement of the strings makes the air move in waves. These sound waves travel to your ears. When your ears pick up the sound waves, your brain interprets the waves as a musical note.

The speed of the vibrations determines the **pitch** of a note. You hear fast vibrations as a high pitch. You hear slower vibrations as a lower pitch. The short strings on the piano sound high pitches because they vibrate much more rapidly than the longer strings. Every piano key has its own string or set of strings (see pages 8 and 9). Each string vibrates at a particular speed to produce a particular pitch.

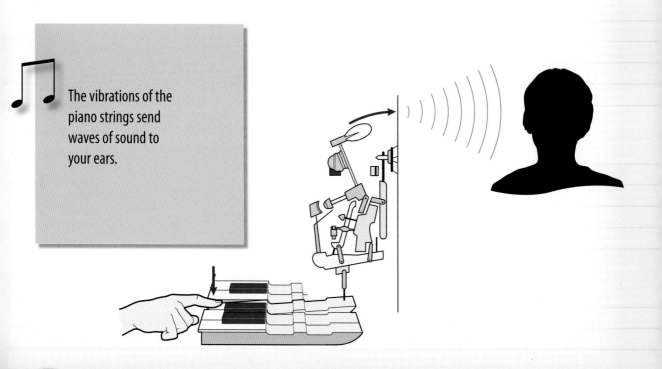

The vibrations of the piano strings send waves of sound to your ears.

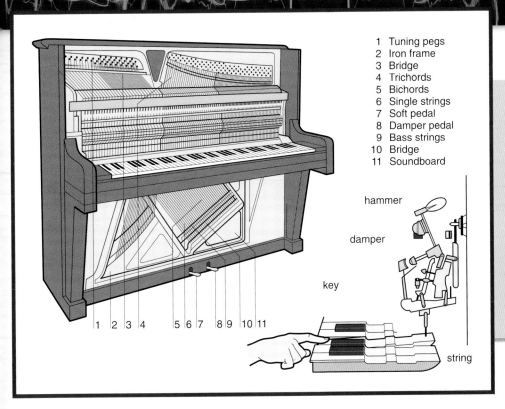

1 Tuning pegs
2 Iron frame
3 Bridge
4 Trichords
5 Bichords
6 Single strings
7 Soft pedal
8 Damper pedal
9 Bass strings
10 Bridge
11 Soundboard

hammer

damper

key

string

1 2 3 4   5 6 7   8 9 10 11

This is the mechanism of an upright piano. When a key is pressed, a hammer strikes the string and creates the note that you hear.

The piano "action"

The piano keys, hammers, and dampers and all the parts that connect them are known as the "**action**." This complicated **mechanism** is different in upright and grand pianos. As you press a key, the damper lifts off the string. The hammer strikes the string and rebounds, making the string vibrate. When your finger lifts off the key, the damper moves back onto the string and stops the vibrations. Try playing some fast notes on the piano and imagine how quickly the action is working!

PIANO FACTS: The piano keyboard

Most pianos have 88 keys. They are always arranged in the same way, with alternating groups of two and three black notes raised above a continuous line of white keys. The notes with lower pitch are to the left. The notes with higher pitch are to the right.

Sitting at the piano

It is important to sit in the correct position at the piano. Your knees should be just under the **keyboard** so that your hands can reach the keys comfortably. Many piano benches or stools can be adjusted to the correct height. You can also put a cushion on the seat if it is too low. Make sure that the bench or stool is a comfortable distance from the piano. You should not feel cramped or have to stretch when you reach for the keys.

Sitting correctly at the piano is very important. Your back should be straight and your forearms should be parallel to the floor.

PIANO FACTS: The third pedal

Some pianos have three rather than two pedals. This third pedal is often known as the practice pedal. When it is pressed down, a piece of felt drops onto the strings. The felt stops the strings from vibrating freely and muffles the sound of the piano. This keeps the music from disturbing the neighbors!

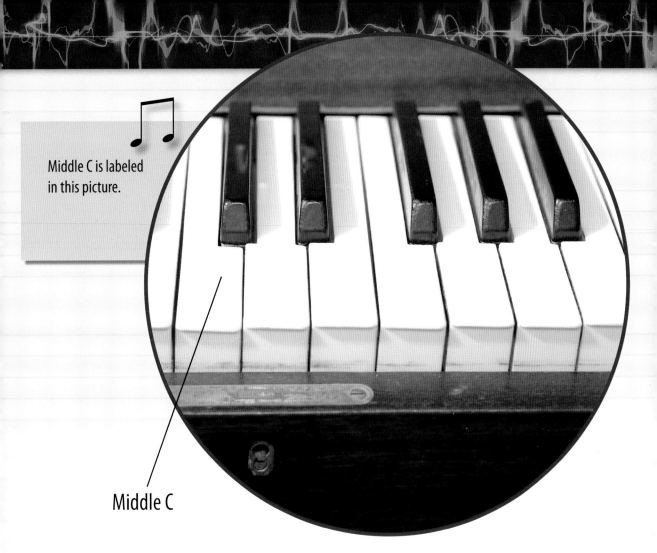

Middle C is labeled in this picture.

Middle C

Finding Middle C

Many people learning to play the piano begin by finding "Middle C." This note is near the center of the piano keyboard. Knowing the position of Middle C can help you find many other notes on the keyboard.

Numbering your fingers

It is important to use the right fingers to play notes on the piano. Imagine your fingers are numbered 1 to 5, with the thumb as 1 and the little finger as 5. Piano music often has small numbers written above the notes. These numbers show which finger to use to play a particular note. For example, 3 indicates the middle finger.

Which Musical Family Is the Piano From?

The piano belongs to two different families of instruments. First, it is a **chordophone**. Chordophones produce sound by **plucking** or striking a string. Violins and guitars are also chordophones. The piano also belongs to the **keyboard** family. **Harpsichords**, **organs**, and **synthesizers** are all keyboard instruments.

The keyboard chordophones

Pianos and harpsichords belong to the keyboard and the chordophone families. So do several other related instruments. The clavichord was popular in the 1700s. It had a quiet, delicate sound. It was good for playing at home, but not for performing in large concert halls. The virginal and spinet were both small instruments with plucked strings. The virginal was popular in England in the 1500s. The spinet was played in Italy in the 1700s.

This is the organ of Southwark Cathedral in London, U.K. You can see the many different lengths of pipe that make up the organ.

The keyboard family

Some keyboard instruments are not chordophones. They produce their sound in different ways. The sound of an organ comes from air blowing through its pipes. The pipes are different lengths. Each pipe produces a different **pitch**. Some organs have more than one keyboard.

The harmonium looks like a small organ. Players use foot pedals to pump air through it. They use their hands to play the keyboard at the same time. The air flows through pipes and makes reeds inside them **vibrate**. This gives the harmonium a wheezy sound.

The giraffe piano got its name because it is so tall.

PIANO FACTS: Giraffe pianos

Many people did not have enough space in their home for a grand piano. Different pianos were designed to save space. The first ones were like grand pianos standing on end. These "giraffe pianos" were first used around 1800. The "lyre" and "harp" pianos were other types of space-saving pianos.

 Electric keyboards and synthesizers do not have strings or hammers, so they are much smaller than traditional pianos.

Electric keyboards

Many keyboard instruments use electricity to produce sounds. The electric piano was developed in the 1960s. It became popular with pop and rock bands because it was less bulky than a traditional piano. The keys are designed to respond to the player's touch. A light touch produces a quiet note. A firmer touch makes a louder sound. **Digital** pianos are a more recent development. (See page 25 for more about digital pianos.)

The synthesizer produces sounds electronically. It can be made to sound like many other instruments. The player controls these sounds using the keyboard and many switches and buttons. Most electronic keyboards can be linked to a computer to record and create music.

PIANO FACTS: Player pianos

Imagine a piano that plays the notes automatically! These "player pianos," or pianolas, were very popular in the early 20th century. A person pumped two foot pedals to drive the **mechanism**. A paper roll with holes punched into it to represent notes drove the **action** of the piano.

What Types of Music Can You Play on a Piano?

The piano has a great range. Its **volume** can be very loud or very soft. Some piano music is very simple. Other more complicated pieces allow a pianist to "show off!" There is more music written for the piano than for any other single instrument.

The piano is equally good played alone or with other instruments. A pianist may perform a **solo** or may play a classical piano **concerto** with an **orchestra**. The piano is an important instrument in **chamber music**, which is music written for small groups. A friendly and fun way to play the piano is as a **duet**—two people playing the same **keyboard** or using two separate keyboards. You could try it with a friend!

The French pianist Hélène Grimaud performs a concerto with the Australian Youth Orchestra. Many pianists specialize in classical music.

Ragtime, boogie woogie, and honky tonk

In the late 19th century and early 20th century, new piano styles developed in the United States. Much of this music was meant for dancing. It had strong, catchy **rhythms**. Ragtime music got its name from its "ragged" (**syncopated**) rhythms. The best-known ragtime pianists were "Jelly Roll" Morton and Scott Joplin. Joplin's *Maple Leaf Rag* (1899) started a ragtime craze in the United States. Boogie woogie also had a fast pace and driving rhythms. *Honky Tonk Train Blues*, recorded by pianist Meade Lux Lewis in 1927, used its rhythms to sound like a train's engine, whistle, and wheels on the track.

The name *honky tonk* comes from the rough bars where this music was first played. The pianos in these places were often rather broken-down and out of **tune**. This style of dance music became associated with the sound of these pianos. Honky tonk music has very strong rhythms. It continued to be popular throughout the 20th century.

The U.S. jazz pianist "Count" Basie led his band from the piano.

Synthesizers are used to great effect by many pop bands.

Jazz piano

The piano became an important part of **jazz** and dance bands in the 20th century. Many jazz pianists of this time are still well known today. Thomas "Fats" Waller became famous for his singing and piano playing. Edward "Duke" Ellington was a gifted pianist and bandleader as well as a **composer**. William "Count" Basie also led his own band from the keyboard.

Pop and rock keyboards

Electronic keyboards such as the **synthesizer** offer many possibilities for creating new sounds and playing around with sounds. Many popular pop and rock performers today, such as Madonna and Moby, include electronic keyboards as part of their overall sound.

FROM THE EXPERTS

"You get that right-tickin' rhythm, man, and it's ON!"

Fats Waller

Who Plays the Piano?

In the early days of the piano, many **composers** were also talented **keyboard** players. They regularly performed their own music. The Austrian composer Wolfgang Amadeus Mozart wrote the first great piano **concertos**. He was known for his expressive playing. In Germany, Ludwig van Beethoven wrote powerful and dramatic piano music. He often broke his own piano when he played!

PIANO FACTS: Clara Schumann

Many women in the 1800s learned to play the piano, but very few performed in public. One exception was Clara Schumann. Taught from a young age by her father, Clara was a hugely talented pianist. She started her concert career at the age of eleven. Later, she married the composer Robert Schumann and often performed his works. She became well known as a concert pianist throughout Europe.

Clara Schumann began to learn to play the piano when she was five years old.

The piano was very popular during the Romantic period (1800–1900). Composer-performers such as Felix Mendelssohn, Johannes Brahms, and Frederic Chopin wrote huge amounts of music for the piano. Performers such as Franz Liszt dazzled audiences with their keyboard **technique**. Sergei Rachmaninov, a Russian pianist, continued this tradition in the 20th century. His many works include four famous piano concertos.

Concert pianists

There were many great pianists during the 20th century. You could try listening to recordings featuring some of these famous names:

- Vladimir Horowitz
- Artur Rubinstein
- Sviatoslav Richter
- Vladimir Ashkenazy
- Martha Argerich
- Emanuel Ax
- Alicia de la Rocha.

Other notable pianists at work today include Mitsuko Uchida and Joanna MacGregor. Mitsuko Uchida is known for her playing and recordings of Mozart's piano music.

Joanna MacGregor is a classically trained pianist. She often works with jazz and pop musicians, including the South African jazz keyboardist Moses Molelekwa.

Jazz improvisations

New names and new styles began to emerge in **jazz** in the 1940s. The jazz pianist Thelonious Monk was one of the founders of bebop. This type of fast music kept the **rhythms** and chords of earlier jazz tunes. It also featured **improvisation**, which is when the player makes the music up as he or she is playing, rather than following written music. Jazz pianists such as Chick Corea and Herbie Hancock combined elements from many different types of music in their playing. Both experimented with electric keyboards and **synthesizers**.

Keith Jarrett

One of the best-known modern-day pianists is Keith Jarrett. He is a jazz pianist, but his interests include all types of music. Early on, he worked with famous jazz trumpeter Miles Davis. In the 1970s he began giving **solo** concerts that were entirely improvised. Recordings of these concerts were best-sellers. He has also recorded works by classical composers such as Mozart and Bach.

Keith Jarrett is a very expressive pianist who is exciting to watch live.

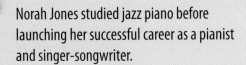

Norah Jones studied jazz piano before launching her successful career as a pianist and singer-songwriter.

PIANO FACTS: Piano experiments

In the 1930s, the U.S. composer John Cage experimented with getting unusual sounds from the piano. He put various wedges and metal screws between the piano strings to create buzzing and other effects. He then wrote music for this "prepared piano." His music sometimes directs the player to use the piano as a kind of **percussion** instrument by hitting the frame.

Pop pianists

Although modern electric keyboards offer many musical possibilities, the traditional piano continues to be a well-loved instrument. Stars such as Norah Jones and Tori Amos perform on stage with their pianos.

How Would I Learn to Play the Piano?

The first step in learning to play the piano is to find a good teacher. Some teachers may visit schools. Others teach at local music centers. Check your local library or music store for information. If there is a teacher locally, try to find out whether he or she is recommended. You could also try looking at the websites on page 31 for lists of teachers with professional qualifications and teaching experience.

Piano or keyboard?

You may already have a piano at home. If not, there are many alternatives to choose from when you are thinking about learning to play. You may decide to start learning on an electric **keyboard**. They are smaller and cheaper than pianos and can be easily moved around. Some electric keyboards are touch-sensitive like a piano. A lighter touch will produce a quieter note and a heavier touch will produce a louder note. Most electric keyboards can be connected to your computer through a **MIDI** link.

Visit your local music store for advice about the best electric keyboard for your needs.

Digital pianos

The most up-to-date technology is found in **digital** pianos. These electronic pianos copy the sound and feel of the traditional piano as closely as possible. They take up far less space than a piano and are much easier to move around. Digital pianos do not need **tuning**. You can also play with headphones on, so your practice does not disturb others. Digital pianos can be expensive, however. Their cost is often similar to that of many traditional pianos.

Practicing with headphones on means you will not disturb other people.

PIANO FACTS: Buying a piano

Before you start looking, decide where the piano will go in your home. Figure out roughly what size instrument will fit in that space. Decide what your budget is. Then, find a good store and ask for advice!

25

Taking care of the piano

The advantage of a piano compared to a keyboard or a digital piano is that it will never wear out or get out of date. With a little care and attention, it will last for many years.

Here are some dos and don'ts for taking care of a piano:

- Don't put your piano in direct sunlight

- Don't put the piano next to a radiator or near a fire

- Do keep the piano away from strong drafts or dampness. These will affect the **action** and the strings

- Do clean the piano case with a soft cloth. Avoid using furniture polishes

- Do clean the keys with a damp cloth, but don't allow moisture to get between the keys

- Don't put drinks on the piano! Spills can cause serious damage

- Do have the piano tuned regularly. Tuning every six months is recommended.

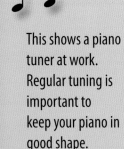

This shows a piano tuner at work. Regular tuning is important to keep your piano in good shape.

Piano tuning

Piano strings must be the correct lengths to produce the correct **pitches** (see page 10). Changes in air temperature can make the strings become too loose or too tight. This alters their length—and their pitch. It is important to have your piano tuned regularly. Ask about piano tuners at your local music store or look in the phone book or on the Internet (see page 31).

Enjoy yourself

Once you have an instrument and a teacher, it is time to start playing. You will probably learn to read music. You will also need to practice regularly. A little practice every day is better than trying to catch up in one long practice! Soon you will be learning scales and playing your first pieces. The most important thing is to enjoy playing the piano!

Playing the piano is enjoyable, but playing with a friend can be even more fun!

FROM THE EXPERTS

"I am a general. My soldiers are the keys and I have to command them."

Vladimir Horowitz (1904–1989)

Recordings to Listen To

Piano repertoire

Classical

The piano has a huge **repertoire**. This brief list gives only a taste of what is available:

J. S. Bach, 48 Preludes and Fugues; *Well-Tempered Clavier*; *Goldberg* Variations

Ludwig van Beethoven, Sonatas; Concertos; Triple Concerto; Piano Trios;
   Diabelli Variations

Johannes Brahms, Concertos; Intermezzos; Waltzes; Rhapsodies; Piano Quartets

Frédéric Chopin, Concertos; Ballades; Nocturnes; Études

Claude Debussy, Suite *Bergamasque*; Études; Images; *L'Isle Joyeuse*

George Gershwin, *Rhapsody in Blue*; Piano Concerto

Franz Liszt, Concertos; Hungarian Rhapsodies; *Mephisto* Waltz

Felix Mendelssohn, *Concertos*; *Songs without Words*; Andante & Rondo Capriccioso

W. A. Mozart, Concertos; Sonatas; Piano Trios; Piano Quartets; Piano Quintets

Sergei Rachmaninov, Concertos; *Rhapsody on a Theme of Paganini*; Études and Preludes

Robert Schumann, Concertos; *Carnaval*; *Scenes from Childhood*; Piano Trios

Jazz

"Count" Basie, *One O'Clock Jump*; *Jumpin' at the Woodside*

Chick Corea, *Now He Sings, Now He Sobs*; *Spain*

Duke Ellington, *It Don't Mean a Thing (If It Ain't Got That Swing)*; *Take the A Train*

Herbie Hancock, *Head Hunters*

Scott Joplin, *Maple Leaf Rag*; *Elite Syncopations*; *The Entertainer*

Thelonious Monk, *Round Midnight*; *Thelonious Monk Plays Duke Ellington*

Fats Waller, *Ain't Misbehavin*; *Honeysuckle Rose*

Modern

Tori Amos, *Little Earthquakes* (Atlantic, 1992)

Keith Jarrett, *The Köln Concert* (ECM, 1999); *Dark Intervals* (ECM, 2000)

Joanna MacGregor, *Counterpoint: Bach/Nancarrow* (Collins, 1996)

Timeline of Piano History

1700   First recorded description of Bartolomeo Cristofori's new invention

1711   First description of the instrument known as *gravicembalo col piano e forte* in an article by Scipione Maffei

1739   Probable date of the earliest upright piano

1767–1791   W.A. Mozart composes 27 piano **concertos** and many other piano pieces

1777   Sébastien Érard makes his first square piano, in Paris

1783   Broadwood introduces the damper pedal

1795   Ludwig van Beethoven makes his debut as a pianist in Vienna

1800   Construction of the first true upright piano by John Isaac Hawkins, an Englishman living in Philadelphia

1804   Challen Pianos make the world's largest grand piano, which is 12 feet (3.7 meters) long

1807   Piano-maker Pleyel founded in Paris. It makes a double grand piano with **keyboards** at either end.

1817   Broadwood presents Beethoven with one of its pianos

1818   At seven years old, Frédéric Chopin plays in his first public concert

1835   Steinweg pianos established. The name is changed to Steinway in 1853.

1848   Johannes Brahms gives his first piano recital

1851   At the Great Exhibition in London, more than 170 pianos are on display

1881   Automatic "player piano" (pianola) invented

1899   First piano competition established in Russia

1920s   "Jelly Roll" Morton makes his first recordings

1927   Kawai piano-makers established in Japan

1940s   John Cage writes works for the "prepared piano"

1960s   Development of the first electric pianos and **synthesizers**

1990s   Development of **digital** pianos

2000   Marks 300 years of piano manufacturing

Glossary

accompany play along with

action in the piano, describes the keys, hammers, and dampers and all the various supports, hinges, and levers that connect them

chamber music music written for small groups to play in small rooms, or "chambers"

chordophone instrument in which sound is produced by plucking or striking a string

composer someone who writes music

concerto piece for a solo instrument accompanied by an orchestra

digital using numbers to process information

duet two people playing an instrument or instruments together

harpsichord keyboard instrument in which the sound is produced by plucking the strings

horizontally parallel to the horizon

improvisation process of making music up as the player plays rather than following written music. This style is often used in jazz.

jazz type of music that was developed in the 20th century in the United States. Its main characteristics include improvisation and syncopation.

keyboard set of keys, or levers, arranged on a board, that are played with the fingers to sound notes

mechanism moving parts that make something work

MIDI stands for Musical Instrument Digital Interface. It is the technology that allows electronic musical instruments to communicate with computers.

orchestra large musical group made up of many different instruments

organ keyboard instrument in which the sound is produced by air flowing through pipes of different lengths

percussion instruments that are played by being hit or shaken

pitch high or low sound of a note

pluck to pull sharply

repertoire music that has been composed for an instrument or group of instruments

rhythm pattern of long and short notes that make up a piece of music

solo musical piece for one player

syncopation rhythmic effect that emphasizes the offbeat

synthesizer keyboard instrument in which the sound is made electronically

technique in music, describes a player's ability to play an instrument

tune when the strings on the piano are all the correct length to produce the correct pitches

vibrate move back and forth

volume loudness or softness of a sound

Further Resources

Books

Blackwood, Alan. *Young Musician: Playing the Piano and Keyboards*. Mankato. Minn.: Stargazer, 2004.

Harris, Pamela K. *Pianos*. Chanhassen, Minn.: Child's World, 2000.

Kallen, Stuart A. *The Instruments of Music*. San Diego: Lucent, 2003.

Thomas, Roger. *Soundbites: Keyboards*. Chicago: Heinemann Library, 2002.

Thompson, John. *Easiest Piano Course*. Milwaukee: H. Leonard, 2005.

Websites

http://www.bluebookofpianos.com/
This website offers information about all aspects of the piano.

http://www.pianoworld.com/
This website offers everything you ever needed to know or ask about pianos, including how to find a teacher.

http://www.learnjazzpiano.com/
This is a site for anyone who is interested in jazz piano.

http://www.ptg.org/
This website of the Piano Technicians Guild offers lots of information and links to help you get your piano tuned and more.

http://www.pianoteachers.com/
This website lists piano teachers in different states and countries.

Index